All designers will know how difficult
it is to find assistants who are intelligent, loyal
and good humoured. We did. And, in
appreciation, we dedicate this book to
Anna, Brian, George, Grant, Jessica and Sarah.

Pancoast — Anderson

Graphic design:
visual comparisons

by Alan Fletcher/Colin Forbes/Bob Gill

Studio Vista : London

Van Nostrand Reinhold Company : New York, Cincinnati

ALL RIGHTS RESERVED, 1963
REPRINTED 1964, 1966, 1969
PUBLISHED IN LONDON BY STUDIO VISTA LTD,
BLUE STAR HOUSE, HIGHGATE HILL, LONDON, N19
AND IN NEW YORK BY VAN NOSTRAND REINHOLD COMPANY,
450 WEST 33 STREET, NEW YORK, N.Y. 10003
LIBRARY OF CONGRESS CATALOG CARD NUMBER 64 - 14628
SET IN 11/13 PT GARAMOND
PRINTED IN THE NETHERLANDS
BY DRUKKERIJ RECLAME N.V., GOUDA
SBN 289 27654 3

Introduction

We were asked to write a book on graphics, but unfortunately we are not writers. We felt we could best express our opinions with illustrations rather than theory.

The vast majority of advertisements, posters, television commercials, booklets and other printed matter clutter our environment and insult our intelligence.

And besides, they are so monumentally boring.

There are, however, some designers and even clients who insist that the public deserve and will respond to much higher standards in graphics. They are convinced, as Charlie Chaplin was convinced, that the best way to entertain the public is first to entertain oneself.

Our thesis is that any one visual problem has an infinite number of solutions; that many of them are valid; that solutions ought to derive from the subject matter; that the designer should therefore have no preconceived graphic style.

To demonstrate this we have selected a number of solutions to advertising and communication problems that are efficient and imaginative.

We have paired contrasting or complementary solutions to similar problems; we hope that these juxtapositions will stimulate students and professionals, if only to disagree with them.

Several considerations have limited our selection.
Designs which required a large format, or used
specific colour not available in this book,
or those which were technically difficult to
reproduce, had to be omitted. We also had to
eliminate many brilliant examples for which
we could not find an opposite number.
With few exceptions we have chosen recent
work so that this book will also reflect the
climate of the sixties.

The credits, which are listed at the end of the
book, presented a problem. One tends to give
either too much or too little information in a
project of this kind. We have given credits to the
problem, to the individual or individuals who
actually solved the problem, and to the client.

The designers represented in this collection
do not belong to any one school. They work
in America, France, Germany, Holland, Iceland,
Italy, Poland, Sweden, Switzerland
and the United Kingdom. They do have,
however, some ideas in common.

Although most of them have done well
in their profession, they believe that design
is not a business but a way of life.

Unlike painters who *should* have a personal
handwriting, designers are often anonymous,
but their work still achieves a vived personality.
Their identity is maintained by a consistently
high standard of problem solving rather
than by a consistent technique or style.

Of course there are always some impossible
clients, but they know that the ultimate
responsibility for a bad job rests with the
designer and not with the client, however

hardheaded and obstreperous. After all, they reason, there are many ways to solve a graphic problem. If one solution is rejected, another must be found.

Each job they do represents a search for new methods of making ideas and images come alive on the printed page; they have enquiring minds and they are not afraid to make mistakes.

They know their craft and use the technology of the graphic arts creatively, rather than being subdued by it. But above all, they never limit themselves to current tastes, or to formal rules of layout, typography and colour.

London, 1963

Think small.

Our little car isn't so much of a novelty any more.

A couple of dozen college kids don't try to squeeze inside it.

The guy at the gas station doesn't ask where the gas goes.

Nobody even stares at our shape.

In fact, some people who drive our little flivver don't even think 32 miles to the gallon is going any great guns.

Or using five pints of oil instead of five quarts.

Or never needing anti-freeze.

Or racking up 40,000 miles on a set of tires.

That's because once you get used to some of our economies, you don't even think about them any more.

Except when you squeeze into a small parking spot. Or renew your small insurance. Or pay a small repair bill. Or trade in your old VW for a new one.

Think it over.

Graphic design is a means, not an end. The illustration, layout and typography in this advertising campaign do not compete for the readers' attention with the provocative message.

No point showing the '62 Volkswagen. It still looks the same.

No heads will turn when you drive a '62 Volkswagen home.

(Maybe an eagle-eyed neighbor will notice that we've made the tail lights a little bigger. But that's the only clue.)

Everything else on the outside is right where we left it in '61.

Inside is another story.

We've put all our time and effort into improvements that matter.

The '62 VW runs more quietly. There are new clutch and brake cables (as well as new steering parts) that never need maintenance. Heater outlets front and rear for more even heating. Easier braking. And 34 more.

One change is literally a gasser. We've added a gas gauge. Our first.

A few die-hards may think we've stolen some of the VW's sporting flavor. But the gas gauge may be more useful than you'd imagine. It will not only tell you whether your tank is E or F; it will prove you're driving a '62.

It could make 1962 go down in VW history as the year of the big change.

The famous Italian designer suggested one change.

Just because the appearance of the Volkswagen doesn't change from year to year, don't think we take it for granted.

Some time ago, we called in a world-famous Italian body designer and we asked him what changes he would recommend in the design of the Volkswagen.

He studied it and studied it. Then he said, "Make the rear window larger."

"That's all?"

"That's all."

We did, starting with the '58 VW.

The Volkswagen is never changed to make it different. Only to make it better.

Changes take place throughout the year. 19 functional improvements have been made in the 1960 VW so far; improvements in handling, in ride, in durability. But your eye wouldn't detect these changes unless we pointed them out. A nice Volkswagen touch is that most of the new parts are interchangeable; they can also be used on previous VWs.

We think the Volkswagen approach to automobile design makes sense. It might even turn out to be the most advanced styling idea of all.

A Volkswagen, obviously.

It's easy to spot a Volkswagen.

Even with enough snow on it to hide the beetle shape.

It's the one that keeps moving.

A Volkswagen will even go up icy hills when other cars won't go at all because we put the engine in the back. It gives the rear wheels much better traction.

That's half the problem.

But the engine can't just be there. It has to keep working.

So we cool the VW engine with air, not water. There's no need for anti-freeze, no chance of the block cracking. (No possibility of boiling over in summer, either.) And there's no draining. No flushing. No rust.

You can park a VW outdoors in sub-zero weather or dig it out of a snowbank; it's ready to roll as soon as you turn the key.

If you happen to live where ice and snow are no problem, don't think you can't judge the VW's extraordinary abilities.

Just try it in sand or mud.

The Volkswagen Theory of Evolution.

1949 1950 1951
1952 1953 1954
1955 1956 1957
1958 1959 1960
1961 1962 1963

Can you spot the Volkswagen with the fins? Or the one that's bigger? Or smaller? Or the one with the fancy chrome work?

You can't?

The reason you can't see any revolutionary design changes on our car is simple: there aren't any.

Now, can you spot the Volkswagen with the synchromesh first gear? Or the one with the more efficient heater? How about the one with the anti-sway bar? Or the more powerful engine?

You can't?

The reason you can't see most of our evolutionary changes is because we've made them deep down inside the car.

And that's our theory: never change the VW for the sake of change, only to make it better.

That's what keeps our car ahead of its time. And never out of style.

Even if you aren't driving the most evolved VW of all.

Our '63.

First you thought small.

And then, of course, someone inevitably comes along and pushes an idea one step further.

Now think a little bigger.

You had the good sense to buy a Volkswagen (or a Renault or a Fiat).
Now you're ready to think a little bigger. And a little faster.

John R. Bond, editor of Road & Track, calls the Peugeot "one of the 7 best made cars in the world." (The other 6; Rolls-Royce, Lancia, Rover, Mercedes-Benz, BMW, Cadillac.) The Rolls costs $15,655, the Rover $3,695, and so forth. The Peugeot 403, however, costs only $2,250* complete. By complete we mean $365 worth of accessories, ranging from reclining seats and sunroof to a silent electric clock.

The Peugeot is a thoughtful car (its 4 doors, for example, open a full 90 degrees; it seats 5 adults in comfort). It is commodious. Quiet. And

on the road, it is one of the great driving cars of the generation. You could cruise all day at 80 (if it were legal).

How long will a Peugeot last? The oldest car still running in the United States is an 1891 Peugeot. The "403" is so well made, it costs next to nothing to maintain; last year, warranted Peugeots averaged $6.50 on parts and labor.

If you're looking for a compact car, why not go to your Peugeot dealer (there are 422 of them) and test drive the only compact numbered among the world's 7 best made cars. **PEUGEOT 403**

*P.O.E. EAST AND GULF COAST PORTS / WEST COAST, $2,333.

FOR ILLUSTRATED BROCHURE, WRITE: PEUGEOT, INC., 750 3RD AVE., NEW YORK 17. FOR OVERSEAS DELIVERY, SEE YOUR NEAREST DEALER OR WRITE: CARS OVERSEAS INC., BOX 158, LONG ISLAND CITY 4, N.Y.

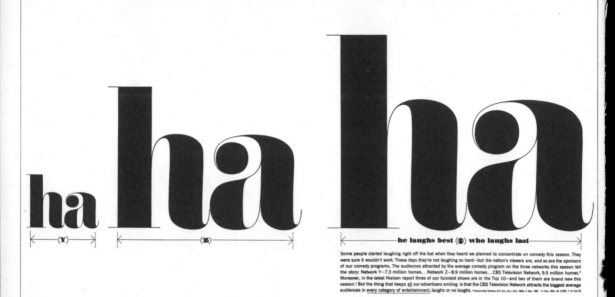

ha ha ha

he laughs best (Ⓢ) who laughs last

Some people started laughing right off the bat when they heard we planned to concentrate on comedy this season. They were sure it wouldn't work. These days they're not laughing so hard—but the nation's viewers are, and so are the sponsors of our comedy programs. The audiences attracted by the average comedy program on the three networks this season tell the story: Network Y—7.3 million homes...Network Z—8.9 million homes...CBS Television Network, 9.5 million homes.* Moreover, in the latest Nielsen report three of our funniest shows are in the Top 10—and two of them are brand new this season.[1] But the thing that keeps all our advertisers smiling is that the CBS Television Network attracts the biggest average audiences in every category of entertainment, laughs or no laughs. *Nationwide Nielsen, 6-11 pm, AA, 1 Oct. 1960—1 Mar. 1961 11 Mar. 1961, AA (CBS: 7 of Top 10)

CBS Television Network

It also helps if the designer has a sense of humour.

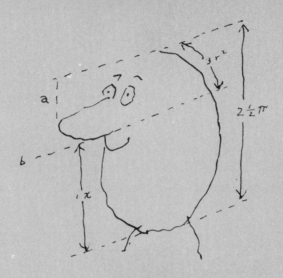

A course in Humorous Illustration will be given by R. O. Blechman at The School of Visual Arts, Wednesday Evenings from 7 to 10, commencing January 30th. Among the topics to be covered in a workshop-lecture series will be Humorous Illustration in Editorial and Advertising Art, Animated Cartoons, Single Panel and Sequence Cartoons. For further information inquire: The School of Visual Arts, 209 East 23rd Street, New York 10, MU 3-8397.

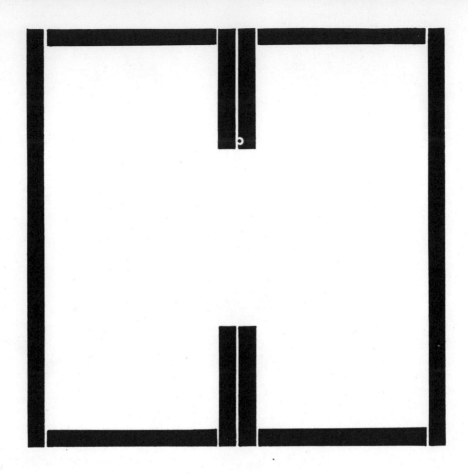

A trademark poses a basic problem. Ideally, it must be simple and distinctive, and must communicate something about the company it represents. This H evolved from the design module of a furniture manufacturer.

This three-dimensional version is architectural; appropriate to a chain of hotels.

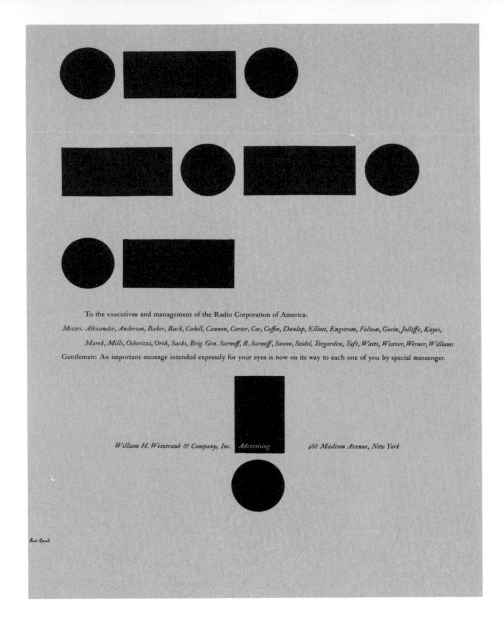

Most symbols have inherent graphic interest. The dots and dashes of the morse code spell R.C.A. Turned on their sides they become an exclamation mark for imphasis, in this advertisement for a radio network.

The seven in this trademark for a film is represented by counting symbols.

SH&L Expanded–redesign of a familiar face. A more flexible version of S&H, long a favorite of people who work with fine design. You can specify SH&L for a wide range of uses from small space campaigns to large corporate image projects. We offer a Bold Face (for impact), Oblique (new ways of viewing old problems), and Casual (no straining for mere effect). For a full showing, call Herb Lubalin at PLaza 1-1250, or write him c/o SH&L, 130 E. 59th Street, New York 20, N.Y.

Repetition ad infinitum can communicate as well as attract.

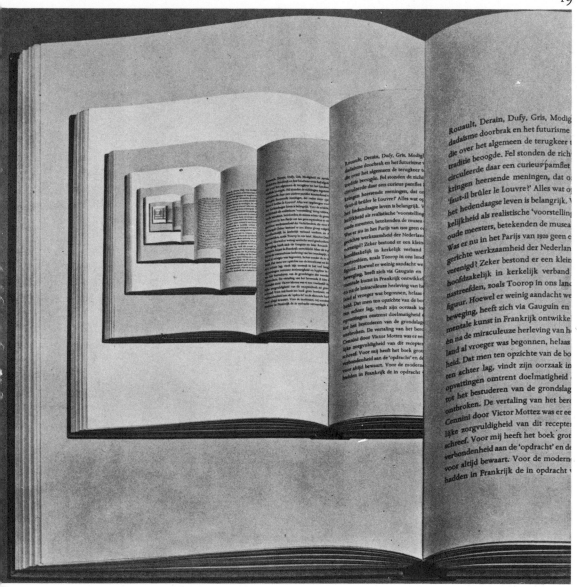

A poster for a Book Fair.

The same object can symbolise different things.

TROUBADOUR COFFEE HOUSE
265 Old Brompton Rd. SW5

If the designer has a strong personality it will come through whether it is transmitted by his own hand. . .

i·wn

or by a machine.

A trademark can be manipulated to create many moods and images.

Our secret ingredient.

© 1962 EverSweet Chilled Orange Juice

The most effective design is usually utterly simple or exaggerated. A blatantly honest orange used in an advertisement for juice.

An honestly blatant sandwich on a poster for bread.

Sometimes the most effective way to focus on a detail is to show its surroundings.

SHOW

THE
MAGAZINE
OF
THE
ARTS
75 CENTS
FEBRUARY 1963

INCORPORATING USA•1

SPACE RACE:
TOWARD
A RENAISSANCE?

MOTHER
TATTLES ON
TENNESSEE

"MAY WE BORROW
YOUR HUSBAND?"
A SHOCKING
NEW STORY
BY GRAHAM GREENE

OPERA VALENTINE: ANNA MOFFO

print

private

secreatary

. . . .

CBS televitsiokn

The designer can make capital out of error. A portrait of the haphazard heroine on a television title card.

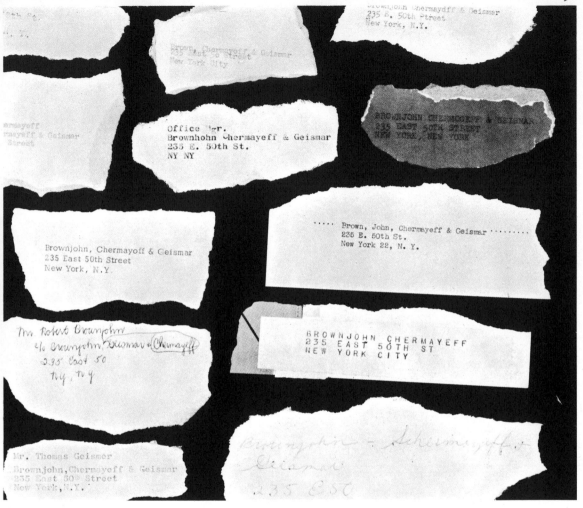

Fragments of improperly addressed envelopes used on a poster to draw attention to a name.

Design, in addition to solving specific problems, occasionally, like painting, justifies itself. A variation of a trademark becomes the illustration in this advertisement.

An exhibition of collage is illustrated on its catalogue cover.

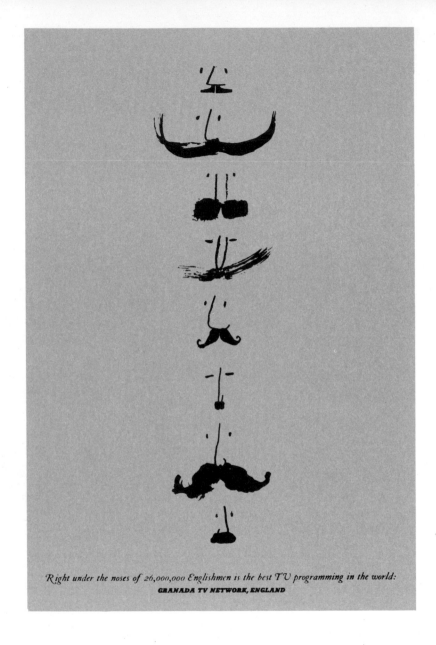

Right under the noses of 26,000,000 Englishmen is the best TV programming in the world:
GRANADA TV NETWORK, ENGLAND

Pictorial detail can re-enforce an idea. An illustration of individuality within a group.

Social comment on the change of an individual

abcdefghijklmnopqrstuvwxyz

At your public library they've got these arranged in ways that can make you cry, giggle, love, hate, wonder, ponder and understand.

It's astonishing what those twenty-six little marks can do.

In Shakespeare's hands they became *Hamlet*.

Mark Twain wound them into *Huckleberry Finn*. James Joyce twisted them into *Ulysses*. Gibbon pounded them into *The Decline and Fall of the Roman Empire*. Milton shaped them into *Paradise Lost*. Einstein added some numbers and signs (to save time and space) and they formed *The General Theory of Relativity*.

Your name is in them.

And here we are using them now.

Why? Because it's National Library Week—an excellent time to remind you of letters, words, sentences and para-

graphs. In short, *books—reading*.

You can live without reading, of course. But it's so *limiting*. How else can you go to Ancient Rome? Or Gethsemane? Or Gettysburg?

Or meet such people as Aristotle, F. Scott Fitzgerald, St. Paul, Byron, Napoleon, Ghengis Khan, Tolstoi, Thurber, Whitman, Emily Dickinson and Margaret Mead?

To say nothing of Gulliver, Scarlett O'Hara, Jane Eyre, Gatsby, Oliver Twist, Heathcliffe, Captain Ahab, Raskolnikov and Tom Swift?

With books you can climb to the top of Everest, drop to the bottom of the Atlantic. You step upon the Galapagos, sail

alone around the world, visit the Amazon, the Antarctic, Tibet, the Nile.

You can learn how to do anything from cooking a carrot to repairing a television set.

With books you can explore the past, guess at the future and make sense out of today.

Read. Your public library has thousands of books, all of which are yours for the asking.

And add books to your *own* library. With each book you add, your home grows bigger and more interesting.

National Library Week, April 16-22

Literal solutions can also be graphic.

a Penguin Book 5/-

Chosen
Words

Ivor Brown

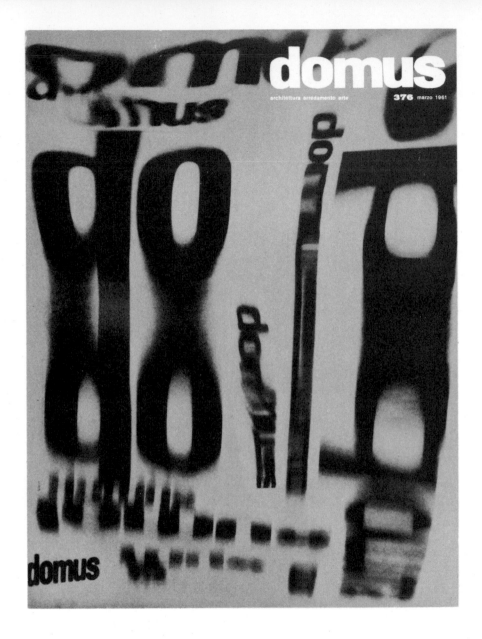

The same design conception can produce different images. Here are two magazine covers solved the same way but with distinctive results.

92

graphic art; advertising art; applied art
freie graphik; gebrauchsgraphik; angewandte kunst
arts graphiques; arts appliqués; publicité

Alan Fletcher

A
WOMAN'S
AMMUNITION
YARDLEY
LIPSTICKS

Objects related out of context create new associations. Lipstick becomes feminine ammunition.

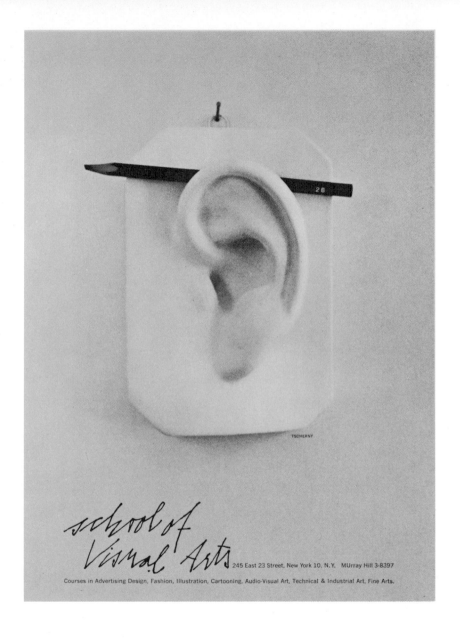

A pencil added to a plaster cast becomes an original symbol for an art school.

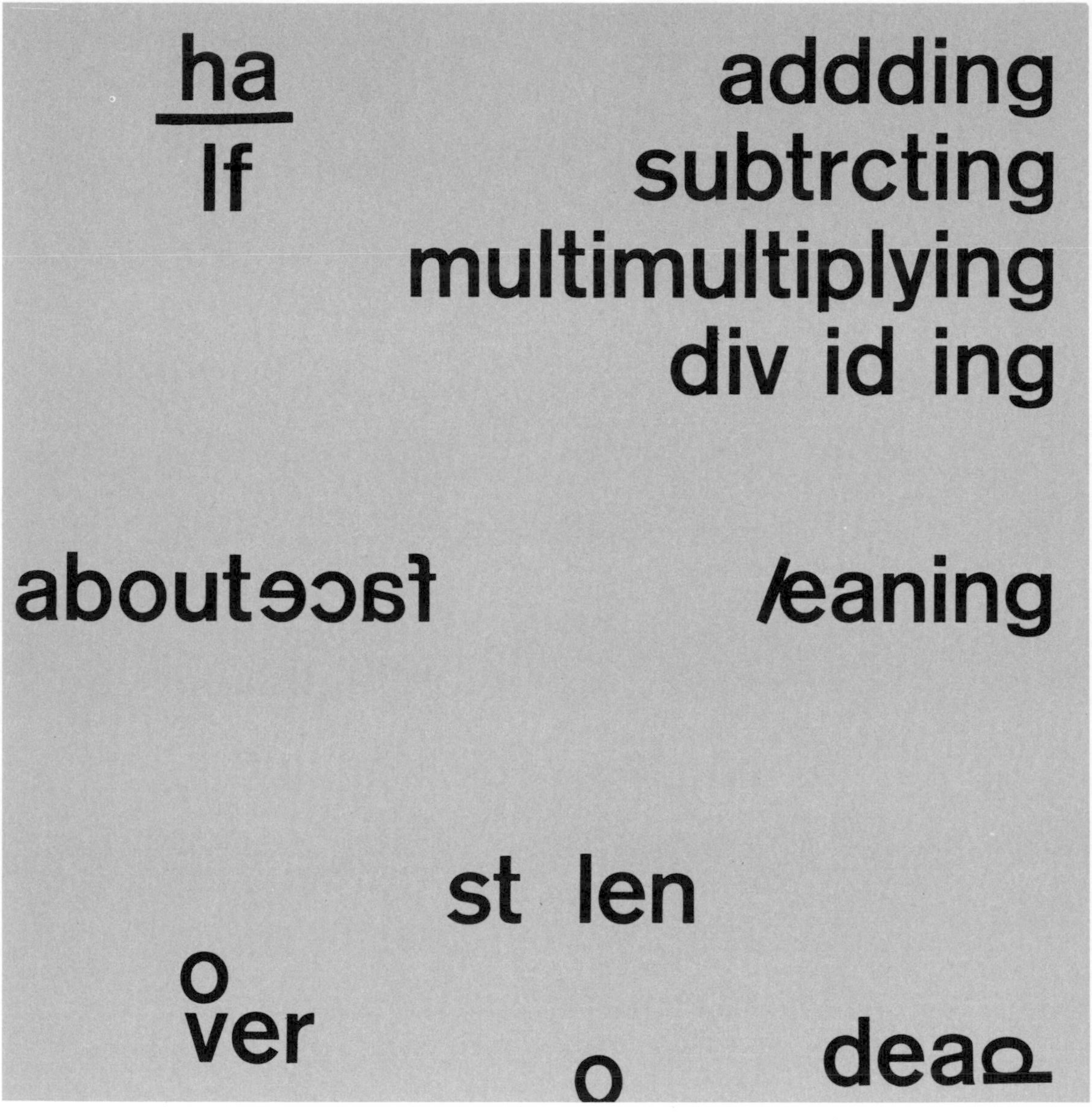
ha
lf
addding
subtrcting
multimultiplying
div id ing
aboutface
leaning
st len
o
ver
o
dea

Type can talk. These exerpts from an experimental booklet are a demonstration of words implementing their content.

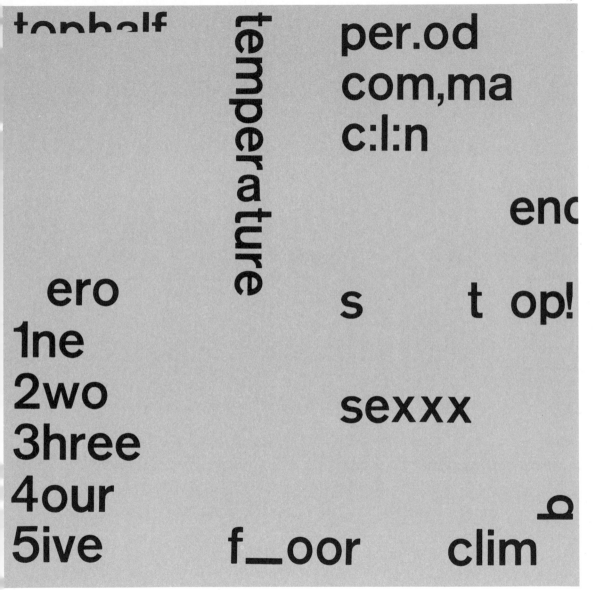

The basic vocabulary of design can be used to create new forms. An experiment with printing rules.

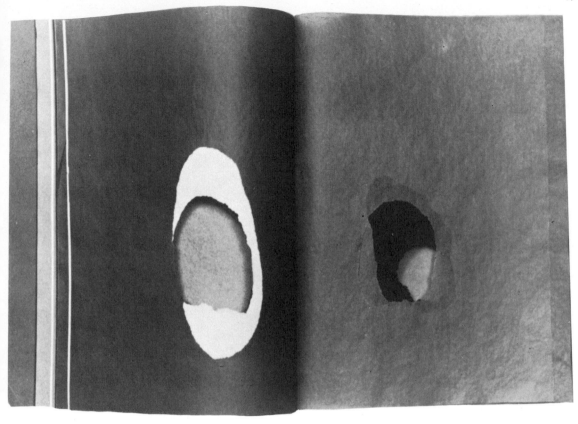

A book without words as a vehicle for collage.

Things which are not essentially visual can be made so.

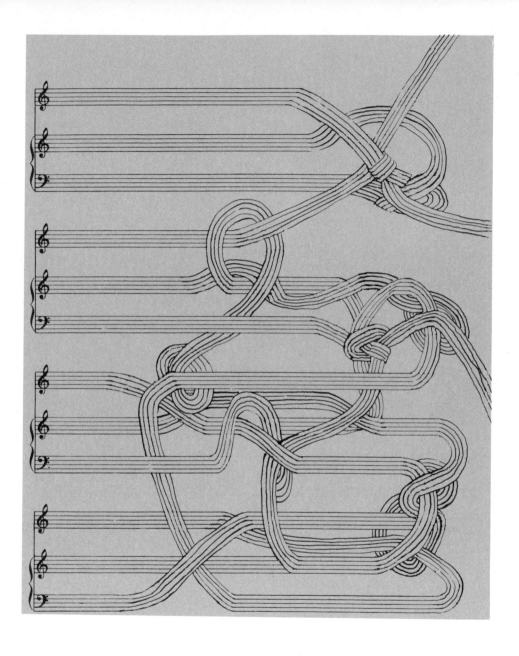

It is possible to *ad lib* graphically. A last minute doodle for a January magazine cover.

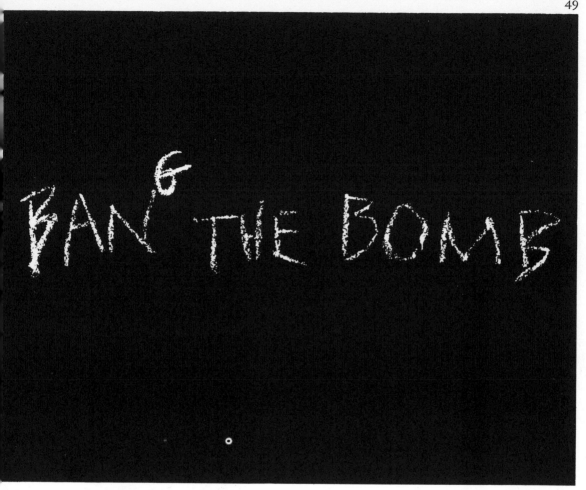

A chalked message for peace on a wall gets transformed.

kunstgewerbemuseum zürich

France   d'aujourd'hui

Art et Technique

Ausstellung	4.Mai bis 14.Juli 1957 im Rahmen des -Printemps de France- und der Juni-Festwochen Zürich
	Montag 14-18 Dienstag bis Freitag: 10-12, 14-18, 20-22 Samstag/Sonntag 10-12, 14-17

Graphic objects which are interesting designs in themselves can rarely be altered to advantage. A poster for an exhibition with the Tricolour.

A set of booklets describing an American election.

get the lead out of your ads A prolific pencil is no substitute for a unique advertising idea. Creativity is an art not a technique at SH&L. Call PLaza 1-1250.

The middle road of design is usually disastrous. Either go wild as in this advertisement for a design office.

or be precise as in this trademark for a process engraver.

Poetry is as rare in graphics as in literature. An illustration for a children's book.

A magazine cover on the theatre in America.

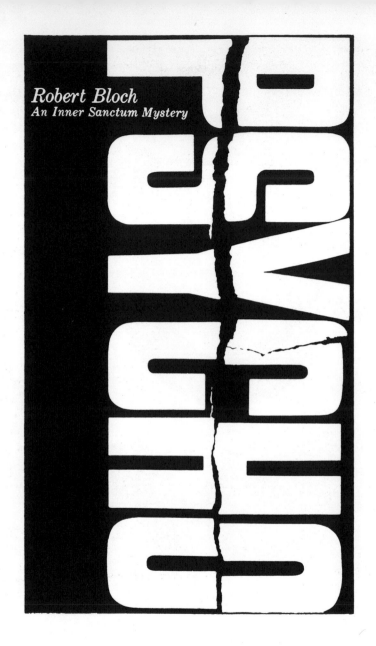

Typography can create atmosphere. . .

ASB ESTO LUX

and describe a product, among other things.

58

Conventional graphics can be used to make unusual backgrounds.

Another full page advertisement made to appear as if the advertiser could afford only a small space.

Graphic solutions should use the environment to advantage. A bus on a poster.

A poster on a bus.

Objects become stylised through simplification. A bizarre image on a book jacket.

A trademark for a television network.

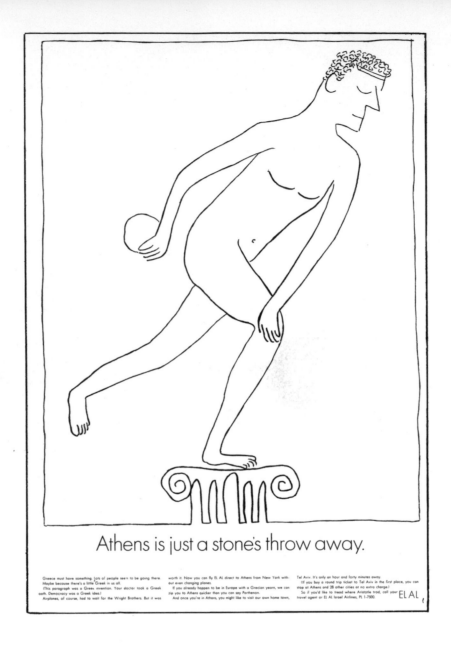

The images of contemporary design come from all periods of art and decoration.

More classical cribbing.

Variety can be achieved with very limited means. A typographic exercise.

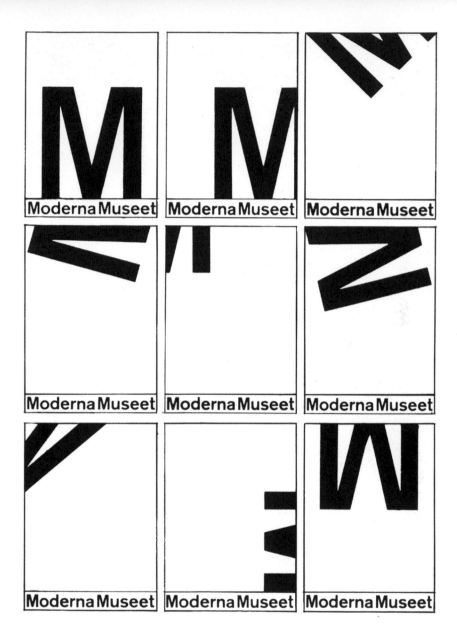

A series of posters for a museum.

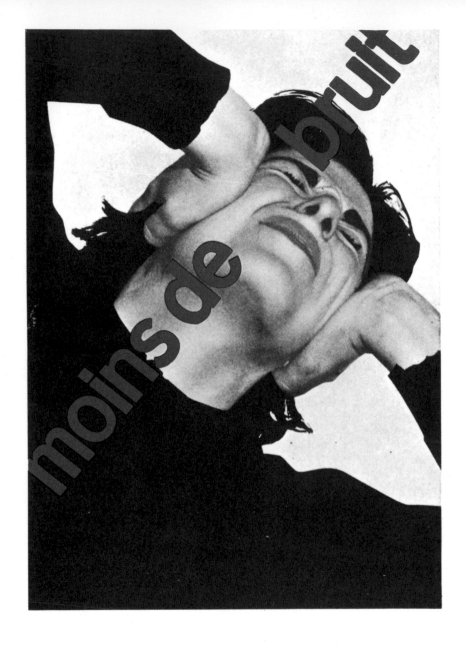

Graphics, in addition to communicating, should be able to evoke an emotional response. A loud anti-noise poster.

A trademark for a sentimental film.

The
HEEL,
said Chris-
topher Marlowe,
was invented by a
woman who was al-
ways being kissed on
the forehead. Undeniably,
it raises her stature, giv-
ing her footing and ele-
vation. This is done not
by inches alone, but
with a sizable meas-
ure of savoir faire.
A DELMAN heel is
a trompe-l'oeil par
excellence. It abbreviates the foot,
lengthens the body, lightens the car-
riage, takes inches off the hips, and gives
the costume altogether new dimension. She
who walks in beauty, walks in DELMAN heels.

An ideogram is a fusion of type into form. It can produce an elegant shoe. . .

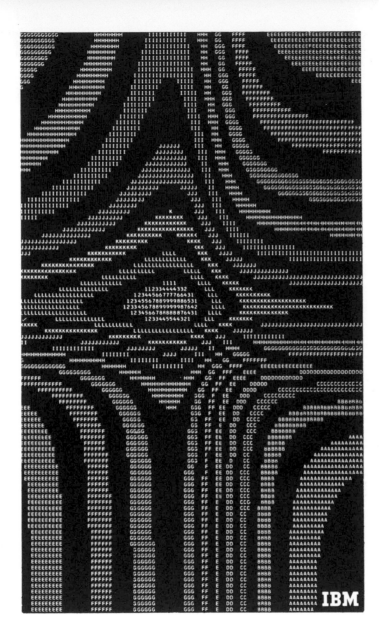

and electronic waves

A primitive solution is refreshing when competition is sophisticated. A magazine trademark is cut in six ways to represent various budgets.

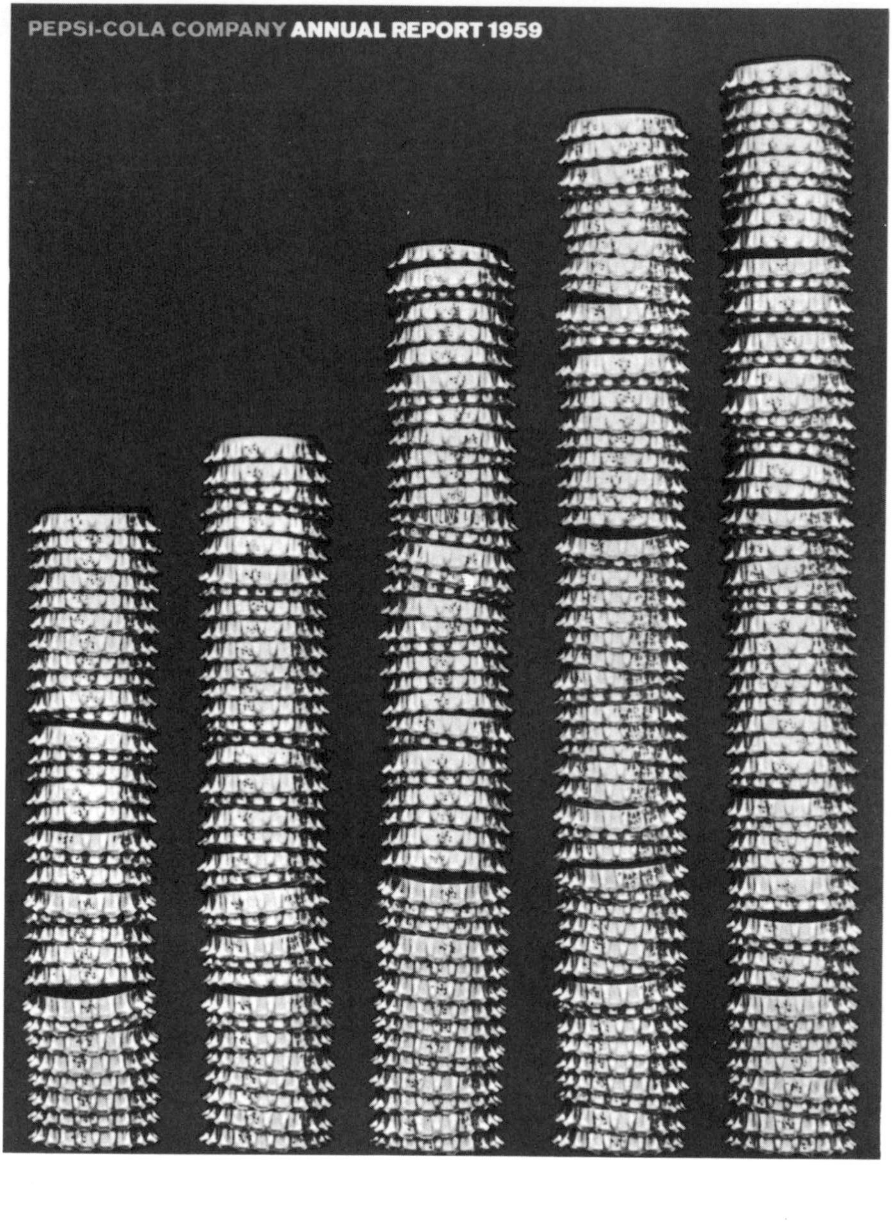

Bottle-tops make a graph on a cover of a soft drink annual report.

Ever since a

RCK

was a stone
and a

RLL

was a bun...

Substitution or addition makes letters superfluous ...

or indispensable.

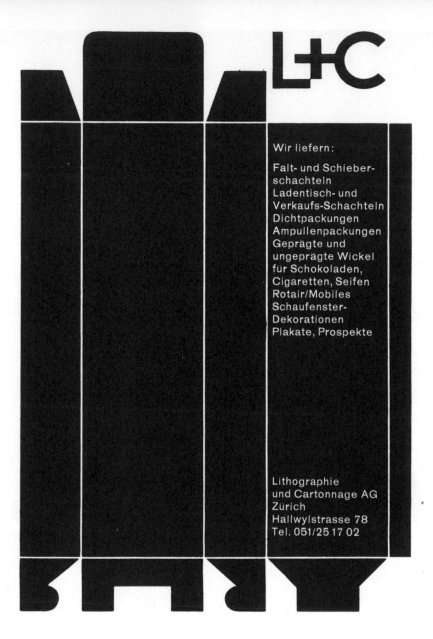

Wir liefern:

Falt- und Schieber-
schachteln
Ladentisch- und
Verkaufs-Schachteln
Dichtpackungen
Ampullenpackungen
Geprägte und
ungeprägte Wickel
für Schokoladen,
Cigaretten, Seifen
Rotair/Mobiles
Schaufenster-
Dekorationen
Plakate, Prospekte

Lithographie
und Cartonnage AG
Zürich
Hallwylstrasse 78
Tel. 051/25 17 02

The character of a product suggests its rigid.

or fluid rendering.

Each problem has many solutions. Here are two interpretations of 'The Americanisation of Paris'. A magazine cover.

An editorial illustration.

Negative as well as positive space can be dynamic. A page from an experimental booklet on typography.

A trademark for a steel company.

Unusual production techniques can be used to support a statement. An unusual fold creates distortion in this booklet on television comedy.

In this announcement of the merger of three designers the binding is split so that their photographs can interplay.

84

Comic book clichés can also inspire original graphics.

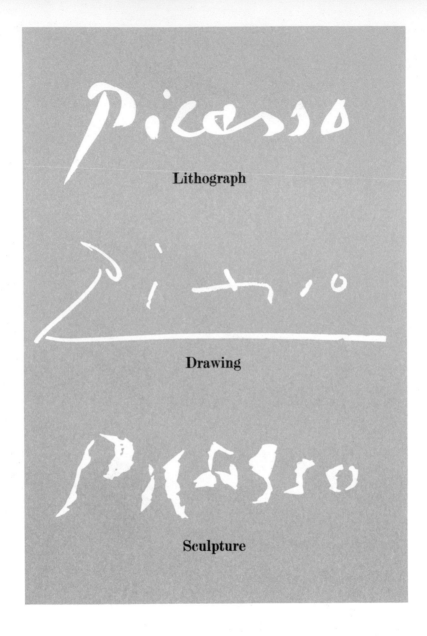

Lithograph

Drawing

Sculpture

Designers should be capable of magnifying differences to make a point. Three signatures of an artist represent three aspects of his work.

One word by three designers for their Christmas card.

two big dates
on your promotion
calendar

Often the parts are more interesting than the whole. The tailors' patterns represent the clothing industry on this booklet cover.

The plastic components of the rose bring out the fact that it is artificial.

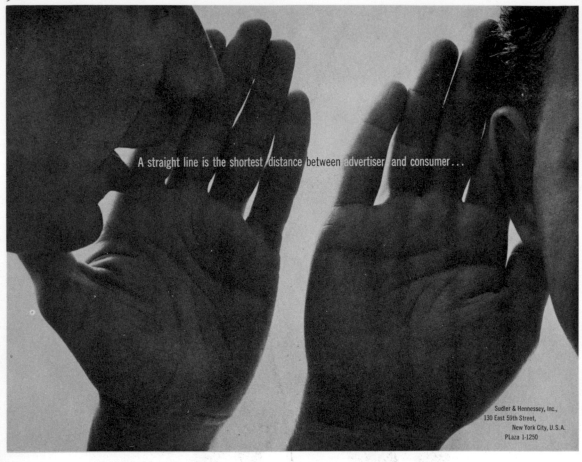

More non-visual material made visual with imagination. . .

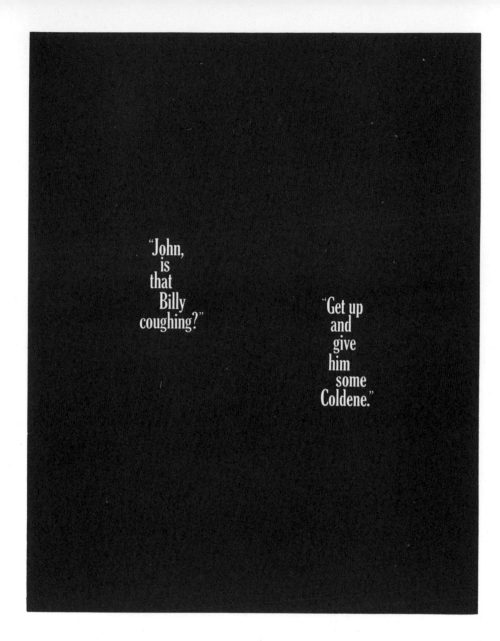

"John,
is
that
Billy
coughing?"

"Get up
and
give
him
some
Coldene."

and some typography.

New trademarks can evolve from standard symbols. Here are two for electrical companies.

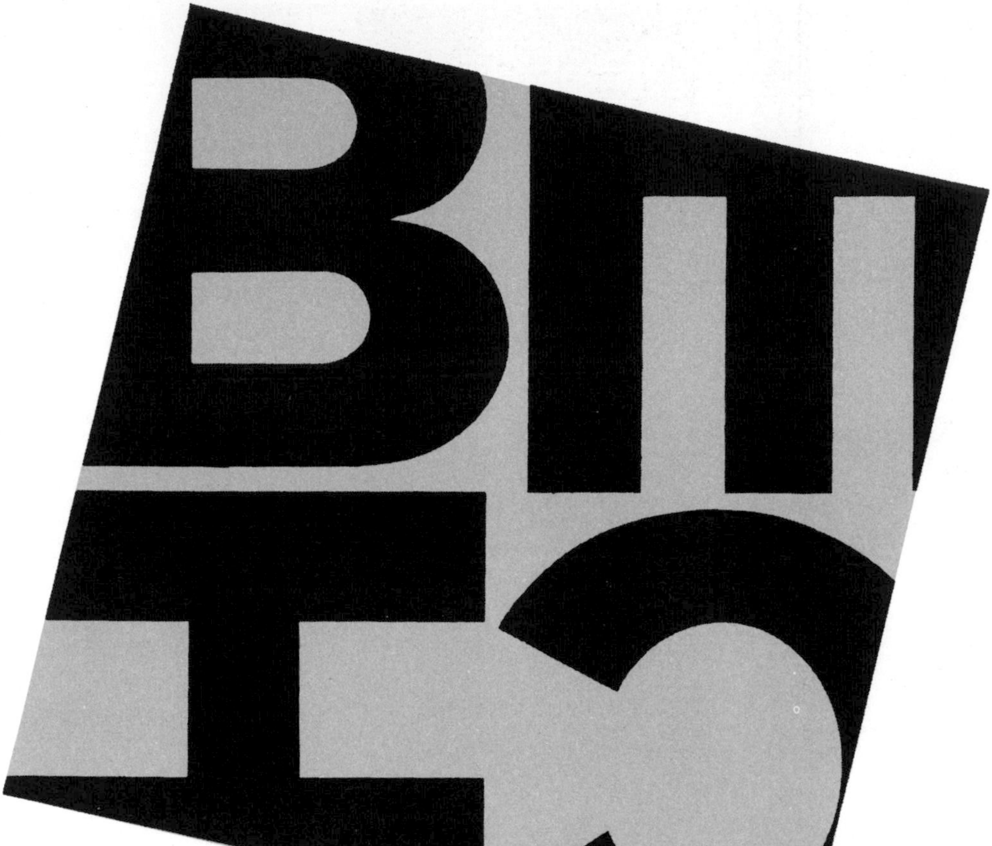

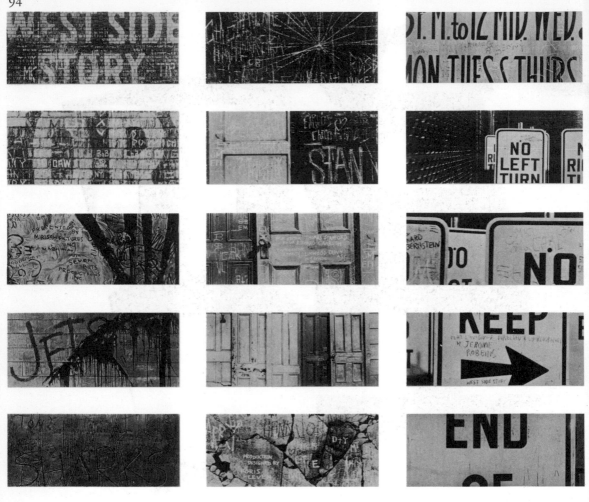

Grafiti and street signs furnish ready-made graphic material. Most designers seem too eager to invent shapes and colours that are far less interesting than those provided by reality. The end title for a film about New York City slum-life.

Credits

We would like to thank
all the above
contributors for their
kindness in allowing us
to reproduce their work.
We would also like to
thank Beatrix Miller and
Lila Karp for editorial
assistance.

Photo on back cover
by Michael Joseph